New and
Selected Poems

Also by Gregory Orr

POETRY

Burning the Empty Nests

Gathering the Bones Together

The Red House

We Must Make a Kingdom of It

CRITICISM

Stanley Kunitz:
An Introduction to the Poetry

Wesleyan Poetry

New and Selected Poems

Gregory Orr

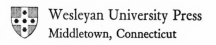 Wesleyan University Press
Middletown, Connecticut

Burning the Empty Nests, Gathering the Bones Together, and
The Red House were published by Harper & Row Publishers.
We Must Make a Kingdom of It was published by
Wesleyan University Press in 1986.

Some of the poems in this book originally appeared in *Ploughshares*
and *Seneca Review*.

LIBRARY OF CONGRESS CATALOGING-IN-PUBLICATION DATA

Orr, Gregory.
    New and selected poems.
    (Wesleyan poetry)
    I. Title. II. Series.
PS3565.R7N4 1988   811'.54   87–13681
ISBN 0–8195–2140–x (alk. paper)
ISBN 0–8195–1141–2 (pbk. : alk. paper)

All inquiries and permissions requests should be addressed
to the Publisher, Wesleyan University Press, 110 Mt. Vernon Street,
Middletown, Connecticut 06457

Distributed by Harper & Row Publishers, Keystone Industrial
Park, Scranton, Pennsylvania 18512

Manufactured in the United States of America

First Edition

Wesleyan Poetry

This book is dedicated to my wife Trisha and to Frances McCullough, for her friendship and guidance.

Contents

from *We Must Make A Kingdom of It* (1986)

New Poems

from *Burning the Empty Nests*

Washing My Face

Last night's dreams disappear.
They are like the sink draining:
a transparent rose swallowed by its stem.

Lines Written in Dejection, Oklahoma

I have never lived on the reservation.
Let me put it this way: in the web of my hands
I hold an egg of air.
When the girl gets off the train
I will be alone. Only myself and
the moon with its rivers and thorns.

For me there is no getting off.
The river writes my name on its side.
The train with my name on it races
over the dark fields. And the Indian
silhouetted against the ridge
lifts his pony, flings it at the moon.

Manhattan Island Poem

Thin river woman with a concrete star
wedged in her ear. I wrap
a blue scarf of old movies around my eyes.
At night I am a jar of fireflies dying.

Daffodil Poem

I remember the cloud on its blue bicycle
gliding over the leaves under the bare branches.
You and I were walking.
You wore your long green dress
with the hem frayed so the loose threads
seemed like tiny roots.
We were holding hands when my hand
became a yellow scarf
and you stood waving it slowly.
I stepped off the train in Pennsylvania,
just as it began to snow.

The Bridge

In the dawn light these white girders
are the bones we want to be free of.

The water calls to me,
saying: Your body is here with us.
Where have you been? We were waiting.
Return to yourself.

Silence

The way the word sinks into the deep snow of the page.

The deer lying dead in the clearing,
its head and antlers transparent.
The black seed in its brain
parachuting toward earth.

The Doll

I carry you in a glass jar.
Your face is porcelain
except for the bullet hole
like a black mole on your cheek.
I want to make you whole again,
but you are growing smaller.
It is almost too late.
When I touch you my fingers
leave dark smudges on your skin.
Each day you are growing
smaller and more intense,
like a drop of acid on my palm;
mothball, snowflake,
dead child.

The Dinner

I invited Mozart to dinner
on condition he didn't
embarrass me.
In the middle of the meal
he began weeping uncontrollably.
"You silly fuck," I screamed,
"what are you doing
in this century
if you can't take it?"

The Girl with 18 Nightgowns

And each one to the advantage of her breasts
which were present in softness
and under softness
were present
like miniature rabbits in the Andes
that only come out at night.

The Room

With crayons and pieces of paper, I entered the empty room.
I sat on the floor and drew pictures all day.
One day I held a picture against the bare wall:
it was a window. Climbing through,

I stood in a sloping field
at dusk. As I began walking, night settled.
Far ahead in the valley, I saw the lights
of a village, and always, at my back, I felt
the white room swallowing what was passed.

"Transients Welcome"

To be like the water:
a glass snake asleep in the pipes.
But behind you the dream burns the empty nests,
and before you the day with its ball of twine.

You piss in the sink. Frying pan in hand,
padding down the hall, you turn the corner
and find an old woman asleep on the stove.

Making Beasts

When I was about ten
I glued together an old
white turtle shell,
a woodchuck's skull,
and a red squirrel's tail
to make my first
mythical beast.
What has been created
is never lost. It crawls
up through my thoughts now
on feet I never gave it.

Poem to the Mother

Dead leaves nest in the crown and the word
"yesterday" is a pile of bones.

But is a volcano ever extinct,
even when its bowl fills with snow
and the giant ice deer come there to die?

Kissing you makes the leaves fall.

How they heaped snow in the cradle
of your hips and it didn't melt.
How at your touch the flowers
exploded in flames.

Again we dismantle the motorcycle.
In your arms you rock the black egg of the gas tank.
A beak like golden pliers tears at thin metal.
Another you is released into the universe.

Beginning

You stand alone in the empty street
and the dark air swept from houses
swirls thickly around your knees.

You remember cutting the white threads,
how a red drop formed like a tear at each end.
But when you cut the black threads, the thicker ones,
there was a sweet heavy smell of flowers and urine.

Now you begin. Because your boots
leave no marks on the hard earth
you will make each journey many times.

Poem

This life like no other.
The bread rising in the ditches.
The bellies of women swelling
with air.
Walking alone under the dark pines,
a blue leather bridle in my hands.

October

At my feet the stream flows backwards,
a road through the hills,
but to travel it I would have to be naked,
more naked than I have ever been.

Behind me the red and orange leaves whisper.
I am afraid of the woods in daylight,
the colors demanding I feel.

My hands are cold. I am trapped
between the woods and the water.
I must face this fear, I think,
and struggle to stay in my body, but
the scream comes, the scream
that is like my hands
only larger, like two wings of ice.

Love Poem

A black biplane crashes through the window
of the luncheonette. The pilot climbs down
removing his leather hood.
He hands me my grandmother's jade ring.
No, it's two robin's eggs
and a telephone number: yours.

Getting Dressed

1.

In the morning, I pull on my helmet of skin
backwards. I see what a light bulb sees
through a lampshade.

2.

Putting on the white gloves,
the ones with little teeth
that close around my wrists.

3.

Pale feet, two corpses that will not stay buried,
I thrust you into my boots:
wearing this barbaric armor
you go out to battle the air, the stones,
the earth that wants to swallow you.

Sleeping Alone in a Small Room

There are dawns when the window is white with moths,
or black with the ink they spin out of their bodies.

I dream of stones covered with snow.
Or I stand on a hill at night,
counting the fires in the valley.
Once I held a blue cup shaped like an hourglass.
Looking into it, past the narrow waist, I saw her
small, child's face staring up from the bottom.

Then there are mornings I wake between darkness and light
and see the cloud that hangs by a rope from the steeple
turn red and begin to dance.

A Parable

The stone strikes the body, because
that is what stones will do.
The wound opens after the stone's kiss,
too late to swallow the stone.
The wound and the stone become lovers.
The wound owes its life to the stone
and sings the stone's praises.
The stone is moved. At the stone's center,
a red hollow aches to touch the wound.
The gray walls of its body tear open
and the wound enters to dwell there.

A stranger picks up the stone
with the wound inside and carries it
with him until he dies.

from *Gathering the Bones Together*

Gathering the Bones Together

For Peter Orr
(1951–1959)

When all the rooms of the house
fill with smoke, it's not enough
to say an angel is sleeping on the chimney.

1. A Night in the Barn

The deer carcass hangs from a rafter.
Wrapped in blankets, a boy keeps watch
from a pile of loose hay. Then he sleeps

and dreams about a death that is coming:
Inside him, there are small bones
scattered in a field
among burdocks and dead grass.
He will spend his life walking there,
gathering the bones together.

Pigeons rustle in the eaves.
At his feet, the German shepherd
snaps its jaws in its sleep.

2.

A father and his four sons
run down a slope toward
a deer they just killed.
The father and two sons carry
rifles. They laugh, jostle,
and chatter together.
A gun goes off,

and the youngest brother
falls to the ground.
A boy with a rifle
stands beside him, screaming.

3.

I crouch in the corner of my room,
staring into the glass well
of my hands; far down
I see him drowning in air.

Outside, leaves shaped like mouths
make a black pool
under a tree. Snails glide
there, little death-swans.

4. Smoke

Something has covered the chimney
and the whole house fills with smoke.
I go outside and look up at the roof,
but I can't see anything.
I go back inside. Everyone weeps,
walking from room to room.
Their eyes ache. This smoke
turns people into shadows.
Even after it is gone,
and the tears are gone,
we will smell it in pillows
when we lie down to sleep.

5.

He lives in a house of black glass.
Sometimes I visit him and we talk.
My father says he is dead,
but what does that mean?

Last night I found a child
sleeping on a nest of bones.
He had a red, leaf-shaped
scar on his cheek. I lifted him up
and carried him with me, though
I didn't know where I was going.

6. *The Journey*

Each night, I knelt on a marble slab
and scrubbed at the blood.
I scrubbed for years and still it was there.

But tonight the bones in my feet
begin to burn. I stand up
and start walking, and the slab
appears under my feet with each step,
a white road only as long as your body.

7. *The Distance*

The winter I was eight, a horse
slipped on the ice, breaking its leg.
Father took a rifle, a can of gasoline.
I stood by the road at dusk and watched
the carcass burning in the far pasture.

I was twelve when I killed him;
I felt my own bones wrench from my body.
Now I am twenty-seven and walk
beside this river, looking for them.
They have become a bridge
that arches toward the other shore.

Two Lines from the Brothers Grimm

Now we must get up quickly,
dress ourselves, and run away.
Because it surrounds us, because
they are coming with wolves on leashes,
because I stood just now at the window
and saw the wall of hills on fire.

They have taken our parents away.
Downstairs in the half dark, two strangers
move about, lighting the stove.

The Hats

The hats are hungry.
What will they eat?
The funny uncle
puts his hand into his hat
and pulls out an empty sleeve.
All the parents are laughing,
but the children are scared.
What will the hats eat now,
the hats our fathers wear?
See the hat in the corner.
Has it been fed?

Like Any Other Man

Like any other man

I was born with a knife
in one hand
and a wound in the other.

In the house where I lived
all the mirrors
were painted black.

So many years
before the soft key of her tongue
unlocked my body.

A Life

At dawn you curl up in the top branches
and sleep.
All day you are a cloud.
Birds fly through it.

At dusk animals gather at the waterhole
as if to drink, but it has become a mirror,
because you are dreaming:

                                At your feet
glass has replaced water, the way
words have replaced feeling.

All night you sit in the tree, listening
to the howl and moan of the animals
in the darkness below.

A Large White Rock Called
"The Sleeping Angel"

He lay down in this field to rest.
Seeing an ant carry
a white egg the size of a rice grain,
the angel believed it was a sign
the animals of this world
wanted to make him their king.

While he slept, sheep licked
his salt wings.
Only these stubs remain.

The King of the Earthworms

Waking each day, always at the end
of a tunnel,
dirt pressed against my face,
I move by taking a bite,
chewing my way through the packed rubble
of earth, roots, and bones.
Like Chuang-tzu's butterfly I cherish
an alternate life: that of a man
who lies down to sleep;
one wall of his room disappears
and the mattress floats out
into the night air.

The Sweater

I will lose you. It is written
into this poem the way
the fisherman's wife knits
his death into the sweater.

All Morning

All morning the dream lingers.
I am like thick grass
in a meadow, still
soaked with dew at noon.

from *The Red House*

End of August

We left our rented farmhouse for three weeks
to escape the heat, returned a day after
our landlord burned down the old barn
at the head of our drive, making room
for his retirement place. A few black
fragments still smoldered as we drove past.
A tractor had pulled the tin roof
flat across the scorched spot
like a handkerchief over the face of a corpse.

The closed-up house was dank and reeked of decay.
We carried chairs and rugs outside to air;
scrubbed walls and floors. Toward dusk I saw
a blue pickup stop where the barn had been—
a young man come to retrieve beams he'd dragged
into nearby weeds. We chatted about a cabin
he hoped to build near the mountains, then I left.
Glancing back I saw him: sweaty, soot-smeared,
a crow moving about the smoking ground.

I grew up among barns. When one caught fire
people gathered from half the county to watch
and talk. I mowed fields in late summer,
hoisted bales into the high lofts.
And played there too: with my brothers
building tunnels and forts, catching
pigeons, walking out on narrow beams to leap
to loose hay. In all that time
I never saw a barn burned on purpose.

A gray sky pressed down as I walked back
to our house. In the front yard two walnut
trees were already loosing yellow leaves.
I thought of T'ang poets writing laments
about their "snow-topped heads" when they
were hardly thirty. All evening I sat
on the porch with a white cloth and my books piled
beside me, wiping blue mold from the spines.

Friday Lunch Break

New York; Virginia

At noon, still wearing their white
plastic helmets and long smocks,
they leave the frozen slabs
of calf hanging from aluminum
hooks on the loading docks
and stride down the street
past my window, headed
for the deli on the corner.
I remember the gray calf we found
last spring in Virginia, hidden
by its mother in a gully;
at six days it scampered
and wobbled. We watched
it grow heavy and slow, until
half a year later, fouled
with its own shit and dull of eye,
it stood with the other cattle
hock deep in muck by the barn.
Then it was gone, perhaps north
to this gallows place, where the men
tromp back, grinning, some with bottles
in brown paper sacks, these men
in spattered white smocks
who are as thick and wide
as the sides of beef they hug
and wrestle, angels of meat.

On the Lawn at Ira's

For Ira and Dianne Sadoff

Six years ago in Ohio we argued free will
versus fate as we weeded your garden
and hosed out a mole tunneling toward corn.
Your father walked out when you were thirteen
and everything you'd since done you called
an act and measure of your will.
At twelve, I killed a brother by accident,
my mother died soon after: my whole life
I sensed as a lugged burden
of the invisible and unforgiving dead.

Now we're sitting on a summer lawn in Maine.
The sun's out; it's the same argument
but I see it another way: you never
let the early hurt be felt and so
it governs you; I now admit I'm mostly
happy, even feel blessed among so many friends.
Hearing a sharp "thump" we investigate
and find a least flycatcher
stunned in the grass below a window.
I hold it in my palm: its small hot heart
beats so rapidly its whole body heaves.
We sit down and continue talking: the bird
lies there with one wing awry, shits in my hand,
stares up with a glazed eye. Ten minutes later
it pulls in its wing, tries to grip
with its tiny feet my too-large finger.
While we talk, joke, and argue
it suddenly flies, unwavering, away.

Swamp Songs

For Trisha

1.

I'm glad when my boots sink
deep in the ooze
and to pull loose, against the smooth
suck, I grab
thick tufts of swamp grass.

2.

On a wide hummock I kneel,
bend close, and watch my numb
forearms and hands: pale
herbivorous dinosaurs
that yank and chew
huge mouthfuls of cress
at the languid delta.

3.

We lie at dusk on the naked
bank, watching as a red-winged
blackbird perches on a cattail stalk
and a muskrat paddles slowly
through weedy shallows toward its mound.

Leaving the Asylum

The metal harps of the high gates
make a clangorous music
closing behind me. They
announce the "new life" of freedom
and only a battered valise
to lug down this alley of poplars.
I repeat the litany of the poem
that released me. Hollow tree
though I am, these things I cherish:
the hum of my blood, busily safe
in its hive of being; the delicate
oily kiss my fingertips give
each thing they touch; and desire,
a huge fish I drag with me
through the wilderness:
I love its glint among the dust and stones.

A Story Sassetta Paints

For My Father

In the background, a saint walks a path
through mountains and a centaur-haunted
forest. In the foreground he's arrived.
He greets a hermit at a cave's mouth.
They've dropped their cudgels
in the stony road, and as they hug
their two haloes are one.

That's all. Let's say they're men,
not saints: what's taking place
is a wished-for, believeable miracle
which must suffice.
When the one enters the gloomy cave
he cannot emerge, nor can
the other, making his way
through the world's woods, ever arrive.

Three Biblical Songs

1. Cain's Song

I was in the fields.
God was a rock in my hands.

From such heaviness
what could rise?

Not his body,
only its cry.

2. Abraham's Song

> And he took the fire in his hand
> and a knife, and they went, both
> of them together.
> —Genesis 22:6

Here there is no light
for the dark to lean on,
as an old man on his only son.

When the wings of the lungs
lift, air enters.

I can't call it hope,
but no blood was shed.

I can't call it grief,
yet the wound won't close.

Much sobbing, but no tears.
Lift up your eyes, God said,
this knife shall guide you.

3. Song of Thomas, called "The Doubter"

Show me, I said, what
my fingers touch is true.

Then a wound appeared in air itself,
like a tear in blue fabric,

and I put my hand
through, into the other world.

An Abandoned, Overgrown Cemetery
in the Pasture Near Our House

March; Virginia

All last winter, starved cattle
trampled a muddy flatness
around it, stretched their throats
over the low stone wall
whose top is set with chunks
of quartz like teeth in a jaw.
Inside, vines cover the five
small cherry trees; brambles
everywhere. And the abyss
with its lips of weather
has already kissed away
the names carved on the stones.

*

I clear it with clippers;
slicing the prickly stalks
and tossing wiry tangles
of briars over the wall
to the cows. It's a warm day.
Working, I sluff off winter's
torpor as a snake sheds skin.
I find a wren's nest, cup
from which ghosts sip.
What's in it? Human tears,
their only food. Always it's empty,
always it's filled to the brim.

The Red House (from a sequence)

Fair seed-time had my soul, and I grew up
Fostered alike by beauty and by fear . . .
—WORDSWORTH, *The Prelude*, Book I

Morning Song

Sun on his face wakes him.
The boy makes his way down
through the spidery dark
of stairs to his breakfast
of cereal in a blue bowl.
He carries to the barn
a pie plate heaped
with vegetable scraps
for the three-legged deer.
As a fawn it stood still
and alone in high hay
while the red tractor
spiraled steadily inward,
mowing its precise swaths.
"I lived" is the song
the boy hears as the deer
hobbles toward him.

In the barn's huge gloom
light falls through cracks
the way swordblades
pierce a magician's box.

Work Gloves

All morning with gloved
hands, we grip and tug
burdock and the tough
fibrous stalks of chicory.
We knock roots against
bootsoles to jar
the clumped earth loose.

When the brushpile's
tangled mound is high enough
we set it ablaze and stand
squinting into the heat,
waiting for the branch
that always rises whole
and flaming, ready
to sprint to where it settles
and put out its sparks
with quick, flat
slaps of our bamboo rakes.

At dusk, easing down
on porch steps to unlace
my boots, I pause:
smoke, sweat, dirt and flesh
make this smell I love:
I hold my face in my hands
and breathe deeply.

The Brave Child

How, on a dare, he would dive where the stream
eddied back on itself, down
to a deepest bottom dark with the rot
of logs and leaves, then like a little
Lazarus rise
with the oozing proof clutched in his fist.

Or, on a ladder nailed to the loft wall,
would climb toward a roof where pigeons
rattled and cooed, hang from a beam
high over hay, then,
with arms spread like a Christ ascending,
fall through the dust-filled air.

Horses

I brace my knee against
one side of the lifted bale
and tug at twine until
it bursts and loosed hay
tumbles from the high loft
over the bowed heads of horses
waiting in the barn's shadow.

In dream, the red one stands
by my bed, wide-eyed and quiet,
though with her mane afire.
Or galloped over quick fields,
it is her neck that sweats
beneath my hand, her sides
heaving between my thighs.

Adolescence

The dog barks from a cloud
after each car passes
and a fine powder settles
on yard shrubs. In late spring
the county truck sprays
oil on the road, binding
the dust. I strip
catkins from willows
and beat the air
with insane intensity.
Reeds bending in wind;
electrical hum
from a roadside pole.
Behind the red house, gray
clouds and the rumble
of summer thunder. Above,
yellow, spiked globes swell
among the deep green
chestnut leaves. And in the hay,
can't breathe; can't
breathe in the hay. Hands
on skin; how good it feels.

Sunday School Picnic:
   What Endures

At the picnic, a fisherman
hauls water weeds and an old
hat from the lake. A whisper
among the charcoal smoke:
"You shall not live forever."
Under bare feet, warmth of pine
needles as we climb
in bathing suits up a path
to the tower; icy damp
of its stairs. We never
touch, we'll never meet
again, but as we lean
together on the balcony, I
glimpse eternity beneath
her pale green suit:
small breasts, pink nipples.

Song of the Invisible Corpse
in the Field

And still I lie here,
bruised by rain, gored
by the tiny horns
of sprouting grass.

I hum the song of spiders
drawing, across the blankness
of my eyes, accurate maps
for the spirit's quest:
always death at the center
like Rome or some oasis
toward which all paths tend.

I am the absence
under your feet, the pit
that opens, toothed with dew.

Hôpital Albert Schweitzer

Deschapelles, Haiti

I pass the old beggar who sits
sucking on a corncob pipe in the shade
of a huge gray mapou tree,
its roots stuck with candle stubs,
gifts for the ghosts inside;

down the hill past the stench
of the courtyard where burros are tethered,
across the parched lawn where kin
of the sick squat beside charcoal
fires cooking rice and red beans;

up the steps and through a double set
of screen doors that never yet kept
malaria out. Mother, I'm coming,
down the halls toward the room
where you lie, coughing and soon to die.

And if I had known, as no one did,
that this would be the last visit, what
could I have brought? All I have:
the sweat and sights and smells
of Haiti under my small straw hat.

Song: Early Death of
   the Mother

The last tear turns
to glass on her cheek.
It isn't ice because
squeezed in the boy's hot
fist, it doesn't thaw.
It's a tooth with nothing
to gnaw; then a magical
thorn: prick yourself
with it, thrust it in soil:
an entire, briary
kingdom is born.

The Weeds

On the lawn, beside the red house
she taught me to slice deep
circles around dandelions
with the sharp point of my trowel
so when I pulled them
the taproots come up too.

She wore a blue dungaree jacket,
her braided hair
tied up in a paisley bandanna.
We crouched there near each other,
mother and son, digging in silence
in the dusk of late summer.

from *We Must Make a Kingdom of It*

A Song

The other world's not for me—
I let my dead stroll there;
pale road, pale throat—
each of its pebbles:
a white, vanishing note.
I far prefer minnow
and mole; I need to know
what their mouths know: round
stone in a stream, heart
buried in a box; to fetch
what's down there, black
and cold as a lump of coal.
To go that deep: ash and tear,
but to come back up: bud and leaf.

A Storm in March

For Trisha

1.

All night rain fell and froze.
This morning I look out
to see ice has covered
each tree and bush, covered
our neighbor's bright blue truck.
The light dazzles and a pink
sap seeps from snapped buds.

2.

How desire outlasts the specific
acts that define it—ash
of the phoenix pyre
compacted to stone—or man
and wife coupling
above their own dust
on the carved Etruscan tomb.

3.

Moving through the cold room
making morning coffee, I pause
to watch a red-faced finch
at the feeder, try to imagine
what he thinks
of this glittering world.
                        It's
about love, that's certain—
this song I hum as I crouch
by the open stove
to ease a slab of oak
onto coals, song whose words
I've lost or don't know.

The Voyages

It's late when I try to sleep, resting
one hand on your hip, the other on my chest
where the rise and fall of breath
is a faint light that brightens and fades.
Today the doctor placed his stethoscope
against your belly and an amplifier
filled the tiny room with a scene
from old war movies—the submarine,
the churning of a destroyer's engines
fathoms above rapt, terrified sailors.
Child's heart, whose thrumming the doctor
pronounced as perfect as such things
can be guessed across such gulfs.

Here, deep in the night, I calm my fears
by choosing a place among Homer's crew,
lolling on Hades' shore. Inland, Odysseus
brims a trench with blood, extorts predictions
from the thirsty dead. But common sailors
already know that launching and wrecks
make the same sounds: scrape of keel on rock,
loud cries. As for the rest,
we need our ignorance to keep us brave.

For My Daughter

1.

This morning holds intact the skeletal
radiance of a dandelion's globe,
bones of delight a light wind
blows apart.
        The winged seeds lift:
a song whose burden is the earth,
lost to us even as we walk upon it.

2.

Desire conceived you: Power
that binds to recombine,
that makes—from dust
and bright-furred beasts—
a risen god, an upright ape.

3.

Love's shrine is strewn with skulls
but where else worship you
through whom we enter the kingdom
of flesh a second time?

Nantucket Morning / *This* World

All night I dreamt of heaven:
a blue space I drifted through, huge
enough to store everything.
                                    Far below
I saw *this* world—pearl
of great price; "Body," Love said,
"is the only boat
from which you can dive to find it."

                    *

Naked, you wade toward shore
through low waves and sunlit foam.
I'm there to wrap a towel about you,
then my arms.
                    Beyond the dunes
whose curve and swell a landward longing
of the wind has shaped, there are leeward
clefts where pink, fragrant clumps
of the old rose, Aphrodite's
flower, take root.
                    And below,
scrub pine woods are already
resinous with morning heat. On a bed
of needles, an upturned scallop
shell, its fluted rim lipped with dew.

Nicole at Thirteen

Grace on which we fix our gaze; pillar
of light that is her lithe, gymnast's
body.
　　　You and I have already passed
the threshold on which she pauses—
how beautiful the naked foot poised
in air.
　　　We've already entered the sexual
dark and now stare back at her, still
standing there as if she could hold
that pose forever.
　　　　　Her bright body
in the doorway—white, lit candle;
our thralled, animal eyes
flashing back from the dark beyond.

November

Unable to sleep, I spend the predawn hours
browsing. Paul talks, in *Corinthians*, about
the Lamb of God: unless the dead are raised
there is no Christ, no heaven. In Plato's
Phaedrus, the soul, imprisoned in a body,
painfully grows wings, longs to mount skyward
toward the world of Forms.
                              But desire's
my god and resides in *this* world,
floating at night on a sea of ghosts
that rises and falls, sorrowful water
pulled by the moon.
                              And at dawn, desire's
there in the white field below my window
where three cows kneeling make small
green spaces around them with their body heat,
shapes in the frost like hopeful boats.

We Must Make a Kingdom of It

So that a colony will breed here,
love rubs together two words:
"I" and "she." How the long bone
of the personal pronoun
warms its cold length against her fur.

*

She plants the word "desire"
that makes the very air
amorous, that causes the light,
from its tall stalk, to bend down
until it almost kisses the ground.

*

It was green, I saw it—tendril
flickering from dry soil
like a grass snake's tongue;
call it "flame"—light
become life, what the word
wants, what the earth
in its turning
yearns for: to writhe and rise up,
even to fly briefly
like the shovelful over
the gravedigger's shoulder.

In Haiti

1. Chameleon

Gripping the small boy's shoulder,
poor-man's parrot on a palm fiber
leash—dust-colored vestige
of a lush world before mountain
forest was burned for charcoal,
before leached soil washed
to the sea.
         Sad land,
the tiny chameleon thinks,
how seldom I need to be green.

2. Sunset at Deschapelles

From the houses of American engineers
laughter and the sound of ice
in glasses. The pastor sets out benches
on the tennis court; it's time to sing
hymns in Creole: "Rock of Ages"
in this land where soft stone crumbles.

Mennonite nurses move through twilight
toward their bungalows. Sweet reek
of jasmine; stench of mango rinds
and urine in the cactus hedge.
Red ants gather on a lizard's eye.

3. *The Palace of Sans Souci*

A mapou's massive trunk
presses against a palace
wall; in a hundred years
both will fall.
                    In his Citadel
on the mountaintop, mad
King Christophe sleeps,
a gold bullet in his skull.

Through which ruined arch
did my family pass?
In a sun-filled courtyard
I call and call.

4. *Waterfall*

Alone with a need he doesn't
understand, a boy strips
by a waterfall no voodoo
god holds sacred.
                    With head
bowed, he stands under crashing
water that downstream flows over
brown-skinned women squatting,
naked to their waists, pounding
laundry with sticks, spreading
it smooth over boulders to dry.

5. *Boy on the Reef / Infinity of Desire*

Three feet below his belly, the reef's
lipped ridge, its last ledge
of coral, then sand sloping steeply
off into dark.
                        Blue of his spear gun
before his eyes, gulp of air
through the snorkel, and as he dives
the face mask pressing tight . . .
                                    Down
through a shimmering curtain
of minnows, past the fish
he seeks, past ragged purple
seafans, past conchs pink as cunts.

Memorial Day

1.

After our march from the Hudson to the top
of Cemetery Hill, we Boy Scouts proudly endured
the sermons and hot sun while Girl Scouts
lolled among graves in the maple shade.
When members of the Veterans' honor guard
aimed their bone-white rifles skyward and fired,
I glimpsed beneath one metal helmet
the salmon-pink flesh of Mr. Webber's nose,
restored after shrapnel tore it.

2.

Friends who sat near me in school died in Asia,
now lie here under new stones that small flags flap
beside.
        It's fifth-grade recess: war stories.
Mr. Webber stands before us and plucks
his glass eye from its socket, holds it high
between finger and thumb. The girls giggle
and scream; the awed boys gape. The fancy pocket watch
he looted from a shop in Germany
ticks on its chain.

Solitary Confinement

Hayneville, Alabama: 1965

Even as the last bars clang shut
and I start to rub the purple ache
clubs left on shoulders, ribs,
and shins, my mind is fashioning
an invisible ladder, its rungs
and lifts of escape.

They've taken the SNCC pamphlets
but let me keep a book
of Keats—poems reminiscent
of my sad, adolescent affair
with the coffin-maker's daughter,
which taught me many things,
including carpentry.
                    And when at dusk
the trusty held for car theft brings
my tray of grits and fatback, it
won't matter so much that, groaning
and puking, I'll be sick for hours.

Imagination is good wood; by midnight
I'll be high as that mockingbird
in the magnolia across the moonlit road.

Poem in New York

The derelict who lives on our street
looks like Whitman as a young man;
this summer he slept discreetly
in a greasy bundle of rags by the alley
trash cans. Now autumn's here, and at night
he sprawls in the warm, sugary gust
vented from the candy store.

*

I sat on the wharf's splintered pilings
and watched the corpse
pulled from the water. Its face glowed
the blue of lapis lazuli.
Two policemen wrapped the swollen
thing in plastic sheeting,
heaved it into the truck
and slammed the green door shut.

*

I listened with the other young poets
that day in the classroom
as Auden, wrinkle-skinned, unresponsive,
recited word for word an essay he wrote
thirty years before: "Your task
is like a mining engineer's—
how to get buried ore out of the ground?
And you can't use magic."

How many times
I've met my double on a New York street—
always he smiled and held out his blue hand
in greeting.

Who, if not he, bends to lift
the rotting body out of the Hudson? Who steps lightly
over the sleeper at rest in his redolent cloud?

Keats

Years ago I worked for a small company making a movie for IBM. In Pasadena, we filmed the control center for the Surveyor moon rocket: at a console I watched its mechanical arm cross the screen to grip the lunar surface. Next we filmed an open-heart operation monitored by electrodes that attached the patient to a computer. I wasn't allowed inside for the actual event, but later, when we returned to New York, it was my job to synchronize the separately recorded sound and picture tapes. I spent hours in a dark room bent over a screen the size of a single handspan watching that same operation again and again, trying to coordinate the sounds that accompanied it (the surgeons' jokes, the clink of instruments in trays) with the primary visual phenomenon: closeups of gloved hands slicing and sewing, the naked heart contracting and relaxing in inaudible spasms before my eyes.

*

Earlier today, as I stood in the Parthenon room of the British Museum, I noticed a woman enter, guiding a blind man. As they moved along the wall hung with friezes and reliefs, she read aloud a guidebook, and what she spoke about the blind man touched, running his fingers lightly over stones carved with centaurs battling human warriors.

At the end of the room they stopped below the East pediment: a huge, triangular arrangement of gods and goddesses whose easeful dignity showed exactly how high above human suffering their immortality had placed them. Where the blind man and his guide paused, the neck and head of the Horse of Night twisted violently up and back as if the angles of stone converging to nothing before its startled face caused it to balk in terror.

When Keats says that this world is not a vale of tears, as religion misconceives it to be, but a vale of soul-making, I believe him. I believe that an act of imagination is one of the ways we make our souls, but it's a way surrounded by darkness and fear. I feel as if I'm in the plane that brought us here to London: all night flying as if not moving at all—as if poised midway between the cold ocean below and the night sky above. But I'm not in a plane, I'm in a small hotel room in the middle of an unknown city in the middle of the night—the room is a little box of light that's not unlike the box with the tiny, lit screen on which I watched the capsule scoop up its ounce of moondust, the exposed heart throb in its bed of blood and fat. Each time I close my eyes I see the blind man place his hand into the marble jaws of the terrible horse.

Going to Meet the Great Poet

For Vasko Popa

In my ten-dollar, Baptist
rummage-sale suit, I stroll
beneath Belgrade's fragrant lindens.

Amazing the number of sermons
this suit has endured:
                    "The body
dies, but the soul lives on."

So do the clothes, though
the pants loved the dead man
and probably wished to follow him
into the grave, though
the jacket he shrank in
has room now to bunch
wings under shoulders
even if there is no tailor
in heaven, no winsome
seamstress in hell.

This suit could be an ode;
serviceable though old,
and of much use
in this world where I am walking
to meet a man who sits
with his elbows propped
on a sun-dappled table,
with his serious gaze
fixed on the lifted glass of wine.

Elegy

For James Wright

Not only doesn't the Ohio stop
tonight; now that your pain
has ceased, it moves more
easily under the stars,
under the barge lights.
And in my veins
blood, though heavy
with sorrow, still flows.
And below the Catskills
the Hudson keeps flowing—
my own river, that's deeper
than anyone dreams
with its rich secret
of fish intact under
all that sewage and grief.

On the Hudson's far shore
there's a chestnut—
my own tree—a plank
fort hid in its branches.
Your poems taught me it
was there, though it's nothing
like your own tree by your own
river's bank—that sycamore,
pure thing so like the simple
word you sought, tree
from which the gray bark
peels and drops until
it stands half
in rags, half in radiance.

A Shelf Is a Ledge

I don't understand by what perversity
Darwin and St. Paul are kissing cousins
on my shelf. And how they both lean against
an encyclopedia of history . . .
It must give them bad dreams.
I watch Saul topple from his horse, but
Paul's all right. Darwin in the underbrush
glimpses a finch. And then there's that damned
history book ticking all night
like a cheap clock while it adds
the day's events to its late blank pages
and erases the early ones so it has
more space . . .
          It's true a sane man
would resist the temptation to animate
dead things of the object world, and
such a shunning proves he's sane. Myself,
I hear a blessed humming in my head
and I'm its glad amanuensis.
Paul's taught me this: Love passes
understanding. And Darwin's on my side
as he implores in the dark: Survive! Survive!

Ovid in Exile by the Black Sea

Ovid's stuck among the barbarians;
he's trying to write his way back
to Rome, though mostly he mopes
along the shore or sulks on a flat
rock in his favorite cove.
He's taken to wearing an ape costume
to keep away the natives. Today he has
another bright idea: to "unwrite"
the *Amores*, i.e., to please the Emperor
with a hymn to Chastity.
                              He's got
the opening now: "Considering how much
there is to say for it, there's so
little that's been said about it. . . ."
The lines begin to flow; he's scribbling
away, oblivious to what's splattering
on the rocks around him: ripe
fruit young girls drop from the cliffs.

For Trisha

The truth's in myth not fact,
a story fragment or an act
that lasts and stands for all:
how bees made honey in a skull.

New Poems

The Demonstration

Democratic National Convention,
Atlantic City, New Jersey, 1964

They bob above us all afternoon—
three giant charcoal portraits
of Goodman, Schwerner, and Chaney,
civil rights martyrs whose tortured
bodies have just been found
in the red clay wall
of a dam in rural Mississippi.

Staring up at their flat, larger-
than-life faces, I envy the way
they gaze at the gray ocean
and the gray buildings
with the calm indifference
of those whose agonies are over.
Myself, I'm a frightened teen-ager
at my first demonstration,
carrying a placard that demands
the seating of a mixed delegation
from a Southern state.
                        No one
prepared me for the crowd's
hostility, the names we're called.

Still, we chant the slogan reason
proposed: "One man, one vote."
And still it holds—the small shape
we make on the dilapidated boardwalk—
reminding me now of the magic circles
medieval conjurers drew
to protect themselves from demons
their spells had summoned up.

On a Highway East of Selma, Alabama, July 1965

As the sheriff remarked: I had no business being there. He was right, but for the wrong reasons. Among that odd crew of volunteers from the North, I was by far the most inept and least effective. I couldn't have inspired or assisted a woodchuck to vote.

In fact, when the sheriff's buddies nabbed me on the highway east of Selma, I'd just been released from ten days of jail in Mississippi. I was fed up and terrified; I was actually fleeing north and glad to go.

*

In Jackson, they'd been ready for the demonstration. After the peaceful arrests, after the news cameras recorded us being quietly ushered onto trucks, the doors were closed and we headed for the county fairgrounds.

Once we passed its gates, it was a different story: the truck doors opened on a crowd of state troopers waiting to greet us with their nightsticks out. Smiles beneath mirrored sunglasses and blue riot helmets; smiles above badges taped so numbers didn't show.

For the next twenty minutes, they clubbed us, and it kept up at intervals, more or less at random, all that afternoon and into the evening.

Next morning we woke to new guards who did not need to conceal their names or faces. A little later, the FBI arrived to ask if anyone had specific complaints about how they'd been treated and by whom.

But late that first night, as we sat bolt upright in rows on the concrete floor of the cattle barn waiting for mattresses to arrive, one last precise event: a guard stopped in front of the ten-year-old black kid next to me. He pulled a "FREEDOM NOW" pin from the kid's shirt, made him put it in his mouth, then ordered him to swallow.

*

That stakeout at dusk on route 80 east of Selma was intended for someone else, some imaginary organizer rumored to be headed toward their dismal, Godforsaken town. Why did they stop me?

The New York plates, perhaps, and that little bit of stupidity: the straw hat I wore, a souvenir of Mississippi.

Siren-wail from an unmarked car behind me—why should I think they were cops? I hesitated, then pulled to the shoulder. The two who jumped out waved pistols, but wore no uniforms or badges. By then, my doors were locked, my windows rolled. Absurd sound of a pistol barrel rapping the glass three inches from my face: "Get out, you son of a bitch, or we'll blow your head off."

When they found pamphlets on the back seat they were sure they'd got the right guy. The fat one started poking my stomach with his gun, saying, "Boy, we're gonna dump you in the swamp."

*

It was a long ride through the dark, a ride full of believable threats, before they arrived at that hamlet with its cinderblock jail.

He was very glad to see it, that adolescent I was twenty years ago. For eight days he cowered in his solitary cell, stinking of dirt and fear. He's cowering there still, waiting for me to come back and release him by turning his terror into art. But consciously or not, he made his choice and he's caught in history.

And if I reach back now, it's only to hug him and tell him to be brave, to remember that black kid who sat beside him in the Mississippi darkness. And to remember that silence shared by guards and prisoners alike as they watched in disbelief the darkness deepening around the small shape in his mouth, the taste of metal, the feel of the pin against his tongue.

It's too dark for it to matter what's printed on the pin; it's too dark for anything but the brute fact that someone wants him to choke to death on its hard shape.

And still he refuses to swallow.

The Trick

I keep thinking of young Dostoyevsky, caught reading forbidden books, talking about unlawful topics. . . . First, he's put in prison, then word comes that he's to be shot. He's hauled out into the snow and roped to a stake, but it's a mock execution—at the last moment a Cossack gallops up with a pardon from the Czar. . . .

It's the sort of event that causes what is called a "break with reality." . . .

In a bar once I heard a story about a warden's bizarre hobby and a prisoner who worked in the carpentry shop. The prisoner lined a coffin with asbestos and pretended to die. That night, guards came to his cell, hoisted the coffin with him inside and carried it out to the courtyard, where they attached it by wires to a collapsed balloon. According to the usual instructions they set the coffin afire so hot air from the blaze began to fill the huge shape.

From his high window the warden watched as the whole contraption lifted slowly into the night air and drifted over the dark roofs to settle somewhere miles away beyond the walls.

The balloon is the soul; the blazing coffin's the body. The trick is not to die.

Tableau Vivant

It's the scene where Hector, reluctant,
leaves for his last battle.
That Achilles' spear will pierce his body
is a promise not yet kept;
it's still whole
beneath his wife's caress
for all its imperfections,
for all its healed wounds
that are like lips held tightly shut.

He hugs his wife. He lifts
his helmet plumed with horsehair
that here seems a child's toy
though in battle it will make him
taller than he is.

A Field in New England

What angel rolled it?
Releasing whom?
                    Where
is the cave?
                Everything
has become invisible
except this granite boulder
that blocked the door
to the tomb.

The Western Invention of
Lyrical Nature

And there's Petrarch, our first
mountain climber, stumbling up
the slopes of Mt. Ventoux
with his shepherd guide
and a bottle of wine—one more
trapped man of the Renaissance
looking for some way out
that doesn't lead to God.

It's almost dusk when he reaches
the summit. He's never gazed
so far, never known there was so large
a vista. He's standing there
for all of us, frightened but brave.
Biting his lip, he tastes the sea.

Live from the Garden

Ladies and gentlemen, I'm honored this evening to be presenting in this very arena, a meeting of giants—a fifteen-round battle between the mysteries of sex and death.

First of all, I want a clean fight, the kind I'll be proud to say happened in my poem. So, as long as I'm referee, you'll fight fair and by the following rules:
No
metamorphosis—if you can't keep your given shape, then clear out. And no stealing each other's techniques, i.e., no "kiss of death," no "slaying with tenderness."

This bout's sanctioned by God not to mention various boxing councils. To put it mildly, it's a title fight.

Death is, to no one's surprise, wearing the black trunks. Sex is, as you can see, wearing nothing at all.

Enough talk. When the bell rings, begin.

Death of the Secret Agent
on a Gloomy Day

The wind was on a binge,
tearing branches with abandon,
seemingly unconcerned
about the damage. . . .
Electricity so weak
it couldn't travel the wires
much less light the bulbs;
I watched it pool
at the base of ceramic lamps.
Then a loud banging
at the back door—it was
a large moth in a mackintosh
and silk foulard. He'd been
badly bludgeoned and died
in my arms, but not before
imparting certain information
which could, had I a mind
to reveal it, topple entomology
departments across the land.

Available Now: Archaic Torsos
   of Both Sexes

Though I'm modest as most,
I couldn't help noticing
certain parts of the statues
have been polished
to a high sheen
by passing hands
as the centuries passed.
If it's a form of worship
it's not much odder
or more perverse
than the saint's stone toe
kissed to a stub by fervent lips.

And even though Plato
suspected art almost as much
as he suspected the body's curves,
he did assert Desire
could lead to the True
and Beautiful.
                    Therefore
I choose to believe that mortals
pausing here to cup a marble
breast or buttock
were doing their best
to grasp the Ideal—
and their foolish gestures
made it shine more brightly.

Carpe Diem: Waking at Dawn

If those clumps of snow we hear
breaking loose on the roof above us
were peopled archipelagoes
about to drop off the earth's edge,
our task would still remain
to grab and hold that moment
opening toward us.

                    Sweet tug
and thrust, wallow and reek
of delight—the world starts here
where lovers celebrate the sun,
that many-petaled flower
poised on the hilltop and about
to blossom, rosebud ticking pink.

The Mother

I was fourteen and it was my birthday party in Haiti. When they brought the cake in, I stood and went to my room. I lay on my bed and wept—the sorrow was real, but so was the calculation my mother would follow, that she would enter and sit on the bed and ask why I was crying.

And I would say my brother's name, he whom, two years before, I had killed, although by accident. And somehow I would have tricked her into forgiving me. But when I spoke his name, she sat awhile in silence, stroking my forehead, and then she rose and left.

So for me nothing was changed. It was as if somehow my brother and I existed inside one of those thick glass globes that enclose a wintry pastoral—two children, bundled against cold, building a snowman while around them white flakes swirl.

How odd for the crying boy to cling to an image of cold in the tropics. At first you think the coldness stands for his mother who cannot comfort him, but you must realize she is also the mother of the dead boy—her son taken violently from her; and how that made her feel no one will ever know, because, in a few months, she herself will suddenly die. At the age of thirty-six to lie down in a bower of ashes.

And I, her son, am older than her now, older than she is in any image of her I carry inside me. So, it must be *my* task to understand and comfort *her*, to tell *her* story, because only I know what's there at the heart of her grief; I see it, no matter what nacreous layers time may wrap it in: a piece of dust, a snowflake, no living thing.

The Hand: "Brightness Falls from the Air"

For my daughter at three months

Maybe you thought it was a bird
or some other strange and harmless
creature fluttering in attendance
as you lay on your back in the crib.

But today I watched as you held
your hand inches above your face,
gazed a long, unknowing moment
then suddenly understood its splayed
star-shape was yourself.

                       You screamed.
I lifted you up and held you close
and all the while I felt you
falling toward our world.

Hotel St. Louis, New York City, Fall 1969

When I went inside, the manager said, "You don't want to live here, kid." And even naïve as I was I could see, looking at the people in the lobby, it was a violent place. I told him I didn't have much money and he said, "This place is for junkies and hoods; go to the St. Louis—that's winos and they're harmless," and he wrote out an address and slipped it under the bulletproof plastic window that covered his small booth.

He was right: in the five months I lived there, no one ever harmed me. I got an 8-by-10 room with a bed, a sink, and a dresser for $15 a week. That left me twenty for food.

My room was on the second floor, with a window on the air shaft. Next door, in an identical room, lived a bedraggled redhead named Beatrice Tiffany and her boyfriend Joe, a security guard. Whenever I caught a glimpse of him staggering, bleary-eyed and unshaven, down the narrow hall in his gray uniform and thick black belt, I prayed he wasn't allowed to carry a gun on the job, or, worse yet, to bring one home. Tiffany's grown son, Eddie, and his boyfriend, Albert, lived in that tiny room too, sleeping on a mat on the floor.

What separated us was so thin it was more like a veil than a plaster wall. Whatever happened in their world happened in mine.

Luckily, we were on different schedules: working six nights a week in a bookstore, I missed most of their family dramas. Mornings, when I was in, my neighbors were either sleeping it off or gone. I'd wake around six, piss in the sink, then boil water for coffee on the stove at the end of the hall.

All morning, I worked on my writing: drafts of poems, dream narratives, stray ideas. Around noon, I'd make two peanut-butter sandwiches, then, in midafternoon, leave for work. In the evening at the bookstore, I'd have a ham-and-cheese sandwich, a piece of pound cake, and a carton of milk. I never varied that routine, telling myself the lettuce in my deli sandwich was the daily green I needed and that the milk made it a balanced diet. Still, I lost two teeth that fall; they simply crumbled and fell out.

One week I was working on an idea to strengthen my memory by going back to the house where I lived when I was ten. Sitting on my hotel bed, I'd close my eyes and be standing on the front walk. To my right was the mountain ash with its orange berries; behind me, to the left, my mother's gray-and-white Chevy parked under the huge weeping birch whose feathery branches brushed its roof. As I walked up the steps I saw the white lattice of the porch and the hole beneath it where the dogs had burrowed. I entered and walked from room to room, pausing every few feet to notice as many details as I could: the worn cane seat of a chair, the color and pattern of a hooked rug my mother had made, the cover of a particular book in the library.

I could only make this journey twenty minutes at a time before my head started to buzz and I had to stop. Each day that week, I repeated my walk, concentrating on a different room and remembering more details each time. There was only a single place—one whole wall of the living room— where I couldn't see anything and found myself wincing and turning away no matter how many times I tried to look.

Late that week I woke up knowing I'd lost control of my mind. Thoughts whizzed by and my head felt light and impossibly intense. This had been my goal—to change my consciousness, but now that it had happened I was terrified. The last small voice of my sanity said: "Don't panic. Get food. Food will bring you down."

I fled the hotel to find a coffee shop. As I passed the super-
market on Broadway, a man in a butcher's white smock
yelled "Watch out!" and pushed by me with a silver shop-
ping cart in which stood the entire carcass of a lamb, com-
plete with blind eyes in a bloody head.

I ate and felt calmer; returned to the hotel, slept, and
woke feeling normal. Next door, I heard Albert telling
Beatrice how he'd walked ninety blocks to the Village to
sell his blood, only to discover it was Saturday and the place
was closed, so he turned around and walked back and now
his feet hurt. Albert's voice sounded flayed and blank as
the dead lamb's face, and I found myself saying out loud:
"How can anyone so dumb survive?" But he did, of course;
we all did somehow.

I slept again, and when I woke it was late that night and
the whole hotel was partying. From all ten floors, confusion
of loud musics and slurred shouts and, in the air shaft, the
whistle and crash of empty wine jugs dropped from a hun-
dred windows.

When I woke from my third sleep, it was morning and I
heard the black janitor with his push broom in the alley,
clearing a path through our jagged garden of glass. He
worked quietly and quickly, and he wore, as he always did
on Sunday mornings, a bright orange football helmet that
glowed like the sun.

For My Wife

In a former life, you
must have been a seal
or so we supposed,
so immune you were
to the coldest water.

Your hair was longer
then and, when you rose
from a dive, slicked
back and sleek
as seal fur along
the line of your skull.

Where did that world
go, those whole lives
we lived each day
when we first met?

It was a secret place
you showed me then—
a clearing
by a spring-fed lake.

I watched from farther
up the shore
while you shed clothes
and entered
into your element.

The Post Office

I'm part of a line in the lobby of the small post office. Some of us have been away for the holiday, others have packages too big for the mailbox. I wait my turn with a tense happiness, a sense of being pressed up against the unknown—after all, it's this brief moment when you can almost believe in that one letter, tucked among junk mail and bills, that will change everything in a wonderful way.

Three people are in front of me: a slender young woman some months pregnant, her magenta parka bulging beneath her folded hands; then a balding, fortyish man; then, at the head of the line, a small old woman in a gray cloth coat and pale pink scarf.

While the postmaster fetches her mail, the man chats with the old woman. Her husband's health? The same—it's been twelve years now that he's been confined to bed. And she herself had open-heart surgery only a few months back. He smiles solicitously at her stories. Her tone is so respectful that, as she takes her mail and goes, I find myself wondering who he is, what position of authority he occupies in our small community.

Could he be the dentist? His clothes don't give any clues. He's not the town doctor, because he was too interested in what she said, too intent on charming her. Maybe he's one of our gentleman farmers, I think, because even now he's receiving his modest pile of mail and almost half of it is seed catalogues. In fact, there are too many of them and he turns to the young pregnant woman behind him: would she like one?

She's obviously pleased. Over her shoulder I see two apples on the cover: one whole, one sliced neatly in half with the bright seeds glistening deep in their white expanse of meat. Then I notice the mailing address: the local funeral home.

So that's who he is, I think, as I wait my turn to approach the lighted window, to receive what was sent me.

The Teachers

Too late, and only because of what happened, we reread the poem and broke the code. And then it seemed obvious the student meant to kill herself.

Tomorrow, I take my three-year-old daughter to visit the zoo. For the first time, she'll see her favorite animals—real lions and tigers. I worry that she'll be afraid, that what she thought was wonderful in picture books won't seem that way up close.

And what will I tell her? These are their real bodies? The bars are there because our curiosities are fatal; they protect us from that part of ourselves that's drawn toward the dangerous life within.

More likely I won't tell her anything, or what I tell her she'll forget. And she has eyes and can see for herself; she has a mind of her own and will decide.

"This is the zoo," I'll say, "where the animals live, if live they can."

The Tree

1.

The word does not share
the world's flaw ("leaf"
is complete, unscarred
by insect or wind-tossed twig),
yet it is an essence
that implicates the world
as a wound implies a body.

2.

Each day the web made new—pattern
of line and space;
                    no matter
how tight the weave, emptiness
at the center.
              No matter how vast
the space, each long-drawn filament,
held fast to leaf and twig, is love.

3.

Autumnal language: fullness and falling
away from the tree of self,
death with a future like seeds
in fruit . . .
              In spring I kneel
to find it: that word in earth
extending downward one root,
upward one leaf . . .
                    Not eyes
discover it, nor even fingers
touching and probing mud, but
mouth and tongue—to taste
this world on lips
where, for that instant, the world lives.

About the author

Gregory Orr won the 1984 Virginia Prize for Poetry for *We Must Make a Kingdom of It*. He has held several distinguished fellowships, from the Guggenheim Foundation, the Fulbright program, and the National Endowment for the Arts. He grew up in the rural Hudson valley and is now associate professor of English at the University of Virginia, where he has taught for twelve years, and poetry consultant for the *Virginia Quarterly Review*. Orr received a B.A. from Antioch in 1969 and an M.F.A. from Columbia University in 1972. His wife, Trisha, is a painter. He is the author of four other books of poetry and of *Stanley Kunitz: An Introduction to the Poetry*.

About the book

New and Selected Poems was composed in Linotype Granjon with Garamont display and was printed by letterpress on 60-pound Warren's Olde Style paper by Heritage Printers, Inc., of Charlotte, North Carolina, and was bound by The Delmar Company of Charlotte. The design is by Joyce Kachergis Book Design and Production, Inc., of Bynum, North Carolina.

Wesleyan University Press, 1987